Countering the Conspiracy to DESTROY Black Boys

Volume Four

Jawanza Kunjufu

African American Images
Chicago, Illinois

7ABLE OF CONTENTS

*I*NTRODUCTION

The Lord seems to inspire me every four years with new ideas about *"Countering the Conspiracy to Destroy Black Boys."* I appreciate the support you've given me in the first three volumes that date back to 1982. I have become very pleased over the past twelve years, with the increasing number of role model and rites of passage programs that have developed throughout the country. I believe it is rites of passage and mentoring programs versus the gangs that will ultimately win the hearts, minds, and souls of our boys.

My prayer is that my two sons along with all African males reach their full potential and become disciplined and responsible in their manhood.

$\mathcal{C}$HAPTER $\mathcal{O}$NE

Mothers and Sons

It had been a beautiful Saturday afternoon and a great game. Before leaving the park, a few of us decided to stop at the restroom. While I waited outside for my nine-year-old son, I couldn't help but overhear a conversation an African American woman was having with her son. He looked to be about four or five years of age. Basically, she was explaining to him how to use the restroom. She seemed to be well educated and very accomplished. Sometimes I like to look at people and see how much I can learn about them in three to five minutes. My first impressions were confirmed while we waited for our boys. We chitchatted about how pleased we were that our home team had won. It was ironic she said, that while today she cheered the home team, soon she would be traveling to the opposing team's city to represent her client as their attorney.

My son came out, but before I could say my goodbyes she asked if I would mind going in to see what was holding up her son, (all he had to do was urinate, she said). No problem, I said, and told my son to stay next to her. I went into the restroom and looked for the boy by the long row of urinals. He was nowhere to be found. I was just about to leave when I saw him coming out of one of the enclosed stalls. I asked him why was he using the toilet when he could have used the urinal. He said, "We don't have one of those at home, and I don't know how to use it." I was amazed. Using the urinal was something I took for granted. At that point I began to wonder, was he the only male child in America who had this problem, or were there other children, especially African American male children, without a significant male influence in their lives?

1

I walked the child out of the washroom and explained to his mother what had happened. I then asked her if I could take him back inside and give him a five-minute class in Urinology 101.

For the last two decades, I have devoted my life to the empowerment of African American people, with a strong concentration on the development of the African American male. I raise many questions, analyze issues, and look for trends that both positively and negatively affect the development of African American male children. The incident at the park sent out a red alert to me. What other rites of passage and learning experiences were African American boys missing under the guidance of African American women who were doing their level best?

The Lord had more for me that Saturday as he prepared me to write this next book. That evening I was scheduled to speak at an awards banquet. The awardees were freshmen entering college. They were spending the entire summer in a science camp sponsored by the local college. The purpose of the camp was to increase the number of African Americans in the sciences. As I spoke, I mentioned how much I respected their work, then I gave them the cold facts: only two percent of the doctors and one percent of the engineers are African American. I teased my audience and asked them how many Asians play in the NBA.

There were 49 awardees at the program, 35 African Americans and 14 Latinos. There were six males, four African Americans and two Latinos. Two of the four African American males would fit the description of a "nerd." One was overweight, seemed to possess homosexual tendencies, and acted very childish. The young man who introduced me, looked like an eighth-grader rather than a freshman entering college, he seemed to possess some physical impairments, including a visual problem that made it difficult for him to read his introduction.

I thought about the sisters in the audience, the numerical disparity, between them and the brothers, and wondered what they were going to do when it came time to select a mate. In my book *The Power, Passion and Pain of Black Love,* I mentioned that if a sister has a BA degree she has a 10 percent less chance of getting married. After completing one year of graduate school it becomes 15 percent and if she earns a masters degree or a Ph.D. or makes over $40,000, then it becomes 19 percent. At the banquet there were 31 females to a mere four African American males. The other two young men were tall, suave, and athletic. I was very glad to see them. I later learned that one of them came from a highly dysfunctional family. His mother is a crack-head and his father is the latest boyfriend in her life.

I began to reflect and juxtapose what I saw today. There was the middle-income African American female attorney whose son did not know how to use a urinal. And there was the African American male college freshman, the product of a crack-head mama and an absent father, who had successfully completed a six-week intensive science camp. It should be obvious that a child's final destination in life transcends race, class, and gender.

In this chapter on the relationship between mothers and their sons - an issue which transcends class - we will examine some of the many challenges facing mothers as they attempt to rear their male children. I am reminded of a conversation I had with a middle-income African American woman. Her son was having problems in school, and she was having difficulty resolving them. Ironically, she was a teacher in the very same school district. Her third-grade son claimed that his teacher was making derogatory comments about him. She wrote a letter to the teacher in order to get her side of the story, as well as to share her son's comments, and she requested a return letter. Three weeks later, having received no response, she called the school and attempted to either talk with the teacher or arrange for a mutually convenient time to meet.

No response. This is one of the same schools no doubt, that encourages parents' involvement and support.

The third time she called she did not ask for the teacher; she asked for the principal. She told the principal that if she did not have the teacher call within twenty-four hours, she would "be in school first thing tomorrow morning." My friend has always believed that the lack of parental involvement is the reason why our children suffer academically. Teachers who have children, especially male children, in regular public schools (vs. gifted or "magnet" programs), have a unique understanding of how challenging it is to advocate with school districts. She told me that the teacher finally called her late that night, and they scheduled a meeting for the following morning. And as she waited in the school office for the teacher to arrive, she overheard a conversation between someone whom she thought was a low-income parent and the school clerk, who apparently thought the parent was not important enough to warrant a meeting with either the teacher or the principal. My friend said that for the first time in her life she realized all that she and her low-income sister had in common. Although one was educated while the other was a dropout, one made over $40,000 while the other was probably on AFDC, one was wearing an expensive fur coat, the other was wearing an old hand-me-down coat, and one was wearing a designer dress while the other wore blue jean cutoffs, in the final analysis, they both were trying to negotiate with a school system on behalf of their sons. An extensive vocabulary, or lack of one, made no difference. They both sat there at the mercy of a school system that held the future of their most prized possession, their man-child.

This first chapter is a response to the large number of letters I receive on a regular basis from mothers nationwide who have either read one of the earlier volumes of *Countering the Conspiracy to Destroy Black Boys*, heard me speak on the subject, or have been referred by someone who thinks that I may be able to provide some direction. I would like to share with you some of the more heart-wrenching letters I have received. The names have either been altered or deleted for anonymity. I think it is imperative that we understand the concern, pain, and anguish that mothers are experiencing as they attempt to raise their sons. This first letter is from Ms. Johnson.

Dear Dr. Kunjufu:

You don't know me, but I have read most of your books on Black boys and I was hoping that you could give me some advice concerning my son. Last week, I attended a staff meeting that was very intimidating. I was the only African American in the conference room. Seated around the table was a principal, psychologist, social worker and teacher, who all used a lot of acronyms - BD, ADD, EMR, and EMH. It made me feel uncomfortable in the meeting, besides the fact that I was the only African American. They were there before I arrived and it seemed as if their minds were already made up when they recommended that my child be placed in a BD classroom, because he has been evaluated as being hyperactive and suffers from an attention deficit disorder. The first question posed to me was, Did I drink or use drugs, specifically during pregnancy? What really baffled me about that question was this child was almost on the honor roll last year and my personal background had not been an issue. I told them that I drink a little beer and that was the extent of my drinking. They went on to say that they felt that my child had difficulties following instructions, completing his assignments, was often restless in class, and was easily distracted. They thought the drug Ritalin would help reduce some of this nervous energy. Dr. Kunjufu, I don't know what to do.

Should I agree to have my child placed in special education? I asked them if I could at least have a week to make the decision. I really felt that the decision had already been made before I had arrived. I simply don't know what to do. Please call me tonight.

5

First of all, it was essential to let her know that I cared, that I appreciated the respect that she had for my work, and that I felt limited in what I could do because of the distance that separated us. I did, however, suggest that she utilize the resources of her local chapters of the National Association of Black Social Workers (NABSW) or Black Psychologists, the National Association of Black School Educators (NABSE), the National Black Child Development Institute, a local teacher's advocacy group, or a sympathetic legal aid organization.

Whenever I talk to mothers in this kind of predicament, I refer them to *Countering the Conspiracy to Destroy Black Boys*, in which I stress the fact that parents have rights. For example, a child cannot be placed in special ed without the signature of a guardian unless the school is willing to pursue a hearing or arbitration. Many times parents are not aware of their rights. I suggested to this mother that at the next meeting she have a representative with her to balance the racial disparity. It's also good for emotional support. As the child had almost made the honor roll in the previous grade, I also suggested that she seek the support of her son's former teachers. Unfortunately, some schools operate like police departments, in that the bond among staff supersedes what is best for the child.

Principals should critically evaluate their teachers before placing the entire onus on the child. Most principals are aware that 20 percent of their staff make 80 percent of the referrals for special education. The problem may be with the teacher rather than the student. I then would ask the parent, did she ask or did they tell her how long they thought the special education class would be needed? What criteria were they using to measure success? I try to point out to parents that presently there is no evaluation instrument to measure the effectiveness of special education.

Before meeting again with the faculty and administration, I suggested that the mother honestly assess her son's behavior by answering the following questions:

✓ How well do you really know your child?
(Games like Checkers, Dominoes, Scrabble and Concentration can help you assess the ability of your child to be focused and follow instructions.)

✓ Does your child have a short or long attention span?

✓ How much TV does your child watch?

✓ What kind of TV programs does your child watch?

The better you know your child, the better you can negotiate the system on his behalf.

I also encourage parents to videotape their child, if they can. I'll never forget the mother who did follow this suggestion. Her child had been assessed with an attention deficit disorder, but the tape showed, without a shadow of a doubt, a child who was focussed during his playtime.

I give mothers a list of questions that they need to ask their son's teacher. Many schools know how to avoid the major issues when they dialogue with parents. One of the favorite lines that teachers give to parents is, "Your son has the potential, but he is not working to his capacity." If the teacher had told the parent that her son was stupid, we would have World War III, but the teacher has softened the blow, and the parent is feeling pretty good. When the teacher says the child is not working to his fullest capacity, the burden of responsibility is now exclusively on him. This is misplaced responsibility. The failure of the child also lies with the teacher and the parent. The following are questions I would like all parents to ask their child's teacher at some point during the school year:

✓ Where was my child at the beginning of the school year in each subject area?

✓ What skills/concepts has he/she acquired during this reporting period?

✓ Where is he/she in relation to your expectations at this point?

7

✓ What criteria did you use to establish your expectations for my child?

✓ How did you make your assessment of my child?

✓ What areas of strength have you identified in my child?

✓ What weaknesses have you identified in him/her?

✓ What are your plans for addressing these weaknesses?

✓ How can I assist in addressing the weaknesses?

✓ Is my child receiving any resource services outside the classroom? If so, please specify.

These are the kinds of questions that place the burden on the person who is being paid to educate your child. It is the job of the parents to assist and for the child to try, but it is the teacher's responsibility to provide a pedagogy, curriculum, and environment that is conducive to learning.

Ideally speaking, the objective for those children who are not in special ed because of a physical impairment should be mainstreamed back into the regular classroom and expected to perform at a satisfactory level. Special education programs should not be designed to indefinitely warehouse children. I also suggest to parents that they query the possibility of the child remaining in the mainstream classroom and that special education resources be brought into the classroom.

Regarding Ritalin, I believe the school system is becoming a larger drug dealer than the Mafia. There are presently 800,000 children receiving Ritalin. Ritalin is a stimulant, an amphetamine. I've always thought it was a contradiction to prescribe an amphetamine for hyperactivity. Ritalin's side effects are loss of appetite, sleeping difficulties, and lethargy. It is my opinion that before

Ritalin is given, a change in instructional pedagogy and curriculum should be implemented. I also encourage parents to visit the classroom, observe their child and make their own honest and informed assessment. If the school is unwilling to make any concessions, parents may have to identify an alternative public or private school, which may present financial and/or residential hardships.

Of all the letters that I receive, the issue of special education far exceeds all others.

Dear Dr. Kunjufu:

I heard you say once that if a child fails a grade between kindergarten and third grade, there is a 70 percent chance that he will not graduate from high school.

I never forgot that statement, and it has me worried now. The school has indicated that they want to retain my child in kindergarten because they don't feel that he has mastered what a five-year-old child should have during this past school year. I believe my child is smart, but of course I am just a mother. The people with the degrees have a different answer, and they feel that my child would benefit from remaining in kindergarten an extra year. They also think that it will make him more mature.

I know that you don't know me and you don't know my child, but I am wondering, what should I do? I don't want children to call my child slow or dummy. I don't want him to wonder why he is not able to keep up with his friends in class. I don't know what that will do to his self-esteem. Please call me collect as soon as you can.

I wonder about parents who express concern on the last day of school when they find out their child has not been promoted to the next grade, when there must have been obvious warning signs during the first, second, and third quarters of the school year. At my workshops, I have parents provide their child's grades based on homework, quizzes, and test scores they have reviewed. When children and parents are expecting an A and the teacher gives the child a D or a C, there is missing

9

information in that scenario that needs to be resolved. Parents who have monitored their child's progress throughout the year should not be surprised in any given quarter, and definitely not at year's end. I also have parents determine whether there was a disparity between the report card and national achievement test scores. If the child has done well in either one, then the parent has an important argument to use for promoting the child into the next grade. Are there regular visits to the library? Is there any reading of stories to children or by children?

What kind of academic stimulation is being provided for children at home? Next, I want parents to give me some idea of how many children were in the class and whether there were any other children that failed. Were there a disproportionate number of African American males retained?

I agree that retainment is necessary if mastery has not been achieved. Society has a right to expect that anyone in possession of a high school diploma can read, write, and compute at a certain agreed upon level. If schools don't enforce their standards, employers will lack confidence in graduates receiving promotions, diplomas, and degrees. I am also against social promotion, i.e. children can only fail a grade once because the school does not want older children to remain in lower grades, or because it is more expensive to educate a child for several years in the same grade, regardless of what they do or don't do in the school year, they cannot fail again. Can you imagine how difficult it is for a classroom teacher to hold children accountable when they know that regardless of what they do, they have to be promoted?

I advise parents to consider their options. As soon as they have a problem, provide additional tutors, at home. We need to increase study time. Privileges at home need to be denied. What my teachers told me must hold true for our children today. They said they refused to allow me to fail. What they meant was that I was not allowed to fail my class and whatever was required of them - extra time, energy, resources, home visits, field trips, inviting role models to speak - whatever it took - to make sure I passed, they would do it.

Lastly, I tell parents that they can appeal to the principal and the school board to have their child "condition" to the next grade. This puts the child on a ten-week trial period, during which time the child must demonstrate mastery of a subject(s) based upon clearly defined and mutually agreed upon criteria. This allows parents one more opportunity to circumvent the problem.

Dear Dr. Kunjufu:

I enjoyed hearing you speak a few months ago in my city. I don't know if you remember, but I mentioned to you after the presentation that I was having problems with my son. He seemed to fit your Fourth Grade Failure Syndrome to a "T". He seemed to be motivated and interested in school in K-3, but with each grade since then his interest has waned. He is now in seventh grade, and he's just completely lackadaisical as it relates to academics. Of course he loves his friends, rap, and sports. I do the very best I can as a single mother (who works nights) to monitor his whereabouts, but I am afraid that at the pace that he is going he may be caught in the wrong crowd and join a gang and drop out of school. I was wondering if you could write to him or give him a call, or possibly on your next visit to my city, stop by and visit. Just give me a call at your earliest convenience. My heart is heavy and I know you understand.

My first question was, Does the child have a positive male role model? And he doesn't have to be the father. There are numerous homes, including mine, where the father is very literate and accomplished, but the children are not inspired to read and take academics as seriously as they should. Many parents tell me that I have said the same thing to their child that they said, but it meant so much more coming from another person. I think it is very important that all children, especially African American boys, be exposed to positive male role models.

Additionally, I encourage parents to have their child read *To Be Popular or Smart: the Black Peer Group*, because peers are the number one influence on our children, and every effort should be made to monitor peer pressure. Parents should know their children's friends and their parents. Get phone numbers, invite their friends over, program the child's peer group with programs that reinforce your value system, and have your children check back regularly when they are outside playing.

I also encourage them to read *Maggie's American Dream* by James Comer, *Gifted Hands* by Ben Carson, watch the movie *Up Against the Wall,* starring Marla Gibbs, and the *Mary Thomas story* about Mrs. Thomas raising Isaiah Thomas. These four strong Black women were able to raise their sons in poverty, squalor, and mire because of a relationship with the Lord and willpower. I also recommend that they read *Family Life and School Achievement* by Reginald Clark, who discounts money or the number of parents in favor of the quality of the interaction between parent and child as the key factor in raising healthy children.

Parents need to review the school's curriculum for its accuracy and relevance. Many times I have sent literature to the school to rebut the fallacy that Columbus discovered America, Lincoln freed the slaves, and Egypt is in the Middle East. Lastly, children are bored only when they are boring people. Parents should help their son find a hobby. Try to find out what your son's interests are and secure reading material in that area. If your son likes rap, subscribe to a rap magazine or get biographies of famous rappers. The children can improve their reading skills while reading material they enjoy.

This last letter comes from the parents of an older youth.

Dear Dr. Kunjufu,

I hope this letter finds you and your family doing well. I've enjoyed reading your work and hearing you speak. I know this is an unfair question, but I'll ask it anyway. What do you do with a nineteen-year-old son who has graduated from high school, can't find a job and simply wants to lie around my house all day long and eat the food that I buy and is too lazy to even help me carry the food up the steps? I threw up my hands seven or eight years ago when he was twelve, and said, I don't know what to do with him. I said that in a moment of frustration, but now that he is nineteen, I really don't know what to do with this boy. I have two younger children that I need to raise, and hopefully they won't end up like him. I'm tired. I have my own life to live. So what would you suggest? Just kick him out? The military? What can I do? Please write or call soon.

In responding to this type of letter, I tell parents about the opposite-sex dynamics. Apparently, humans in Western countries are not skilled at pushing their children out of the nest, as Eastern countries and in the animal kingdom. It is a greater challenge when the opposite gender is involved. Mothers seem to do a much better job of preparing their daughters to leave than their sons. Fathers seem to do a much better job with their sons than their daughters. We have a rule at our house: we will give you everything you *need* for the first eighteen years of your life, and on your eighteenth birthday you must leave, preferably for college. Parents are in a dilemma when they know their son may not be college material or may not be serious about his future. Who wants to spend $10,000 - 15,000 a year for a student who's not serious? It is mind boggling when you consider that children receiving money from parents for one to three years may not do well; when the money is cut, and the students are forced to pay their own way through school, they seem to do much better.

Many of our youth believe that the worst scenario or consequence that could happen to them if they can't provide their living accommodations is that they will remain in the parent's home. They believe that staying at home is a viable option. This allows them to play grownup while acting like children. Many youth, because of materialism, want to remain in their parents' house while they spend their money on Western trinkets instead of rent, utilities, and food. This, in my opinion, can deceive children about reality. I wish there was an institution similar to a dormitory where parents could send unmotivated youth who want to be grownup but can't pay for it.

Our mother mentioned that her son is unemployed, and I'm wondering how aggressively he has been looking for employment. Mothers need to put the fire under their sons and let them know that their stay cannot be indefinite. Obviously, if a person did not have a support system, he'd have to look day-by-day, if not hour-by-hour, and accept whatever was available. As we have allowed our children to become irresponsible, they often don't feel compelled to accept a minimum wage job, wash dishes, or be involved in commission sales.

The military option is more complex. There are many mothers who have used the military to teach their sons responsibility, and have been successful. I am concerned about how parents can say I don't know what to do with him after eighteen years and expect the military to teach them discipline in two to three months. I could give you horror stories on the abuse and the disproportionate number of African American males who have received a dishonorable discharge, which can effect their employment opportunities for the rest of their lives. I could also mention to you studies illustrating that the military has been fairer to African American males than corporate America. Colin Powell showed us that there is no glass ceiling in the military, in contrast to the Fortune 500. That does not mean that racism does not exist in the military. African American males are only six percent of the population, but they are one-third of the military. There remains a disproportionate percentage of African American males on the front-line, and involved in combat duty. I am not concerned only with our sons being on the front-line, but especially in places like Haiti, Rwanda, Liberia, and Nigeria. In a world based on white supremacy, African males from various countries don't need to kill each other to maintain the oppression of its people. I encourage mothers to attend the registration meetings with the military and monitor the application. If your son has expressed an interest in electronics, aviation, or another technical field that is noncombative, every effort should be made to attain that reality.

I usually close my letters or conversations by imploring the mother to stay strong and give her son tough love. I remember my father telling me that if I ever got locked up he was not going to get me out. My mother said she would, but my father told her "Don't even think about it." I knew he meant it, and even though I didn't like what he said, I am raising my sons by similar rules. For many parents the problem is the lack of rules. For others, it's the ability to enforce them. If the consequence of breaking the rules is kicking the child out of the house, then you must be prepared to follow through. With the streets as dangerous as they are, mothers are reluctant to have their sons leave and become the victim of an act of violence that she will always think was her fault and could have been prevented. It's the choice between a rock and a hard place. If the rock is allowing my son to stay home and be irresponsible, and the hard place is taking the chance that my son will be a victim of an act of violence, I'm going to take the hard place, because it is the only hope for teaching responsibility. If mothers allow their sons to stay with them irresponsibly, they may be physically alive but they are mentally, emotionally, financially, and spiritually bankrupt and dead. When our mother said that her son eats up all the food in her house, yet was too lazy to help her carry the food, in my opinion, death has already begun.

I wish mothers of sons could have a conference and benefit and derive strength from each other. Mothers are worrying about and suffering from similar problems. They are responding individually without support; they are waiting in school offices by themselves. They are arguing with school clerks, teachers, and principals by themselves. They are meeting with four professionals about their son's future, by themselves. They are tackling lack of motivation, peer pressure, gangs and other vices by themselves.

In many cities mothers who have buried their sons due to wanton violence have organized themselves into various groups: Mothers against Gangs, Mothers against Violence, Mothers against Crime. Most had not considered getting together until a tragedy happened to their son. I commend them for coming together to try to prevent another child from being a victim. I wish we could organize mothers before their sons' lives are snuffed out at an early age. Not only do we need Mothers against Gangs, we need Mothers against Ritalin, Mothers against a Disproportionate Number of Black Boys Failing Kindergarten, Mothers against Special Education, Mothers against Teachers That Give Our Boys Low Expectations, and Mothers against Gangster Rap.

In this chapter I have attempted to portray some of the concerns that mothers have in raising their sons. In the next chapter we will look at what an African American male high school graduate must do in a postindustrial economy.

$\mathcal{C}$HAPTER $\mathcal{T}$WO

Diploma and Entropy

It was a big day for the Taylors, for today their only son Marlon was graduating from high school. It was nearing seven o'clock in the evening, and the limousine was waiting outside for the Taylor clan. It had been a very special year for Marlon. He had attended the senior prom in the same limousine. It was a beautiful white Lincoln stretch with large whitewall tires, a TV, VCR, CD player, and telephone. Mr. and Mrs. Taylor were very proud of their son. He had accomplished far beyond what they had been able to achieve. Family members from around the state had traveled to attend this very special event. Some had already gone to the school, but others wanted to come to the house and take a few pregraduation pictures and maybe ride in the limousine. Marlon was upstairs putting on his white suit jacket (which just so happened to match the limousine), and he combed his hair for the twenty-seventh time.

When Marlon was finally satisfied, he came downstairs. You would have thought that he was Mandela from South Africa or the President of the United States. A total of eleven people climbed into that limousine for the ride to Frederick Douglass High School.

The family had much to be proud of. Four years ago 300 freshmen had entered the school, 150 male and 150 female. Four years later, only 200 students were graduating, 125 females and 75 males, and Marlon Taylor was one of them.

When they arrived at the high school, they took more pictures. The Taylor family was not alone with their red carpet treatment. Graduation day is a big occasion for most families in this city.

After a few more minutes of picture taking, the Taylor family entered the auditorium and tried to get seats close to the front. Marlon went into the room with his graduating class. The principal, Mrs. Roberts, and the assistant principal, Mr. Johnson, along with faculty and other staff, were assisting students with their caps and gowns. Marlon was teasing some of the sisters and playing with the brothers and everybody seemed to be in a warm and jovial spirit. The organist cued the students to line up for the procession. They lined up, first by divisions and second by height.

"I now introduce to you the Douglass class of 1994."

There was a deafening roar from the crowd; there was a standing ovation as 200 proud African American students walked down the aisle. The graduation exercise included the Pledge of Allegiance, "Lift Every Voice and Sing," and an opening prayer. There were several songs, a welcoming, and speeches by the valedictorian and salutatorian. There was a special guest speaker, and then Mrs. Roberts came to the microphone and said, "And now the moment we have been waiting for. We now present the graduates. We ask that parents wait until all graduates have received their diploma and then we will give them a strong round of applause."

The students giggled because they knew that their families were going to shout, applaud, and take pictures anyway. The presentation of graduates was a big popularity contest; whomever had secured the most tickets would receive the loudest applause. The Taylor family had twenty-six people. Marlon couldn't wait for his name to be called. He wished his name was Marlon Allen so that his name could be called first, but since his last name was Taylor, he'd have to wait a while. He had waited four years, so twenty additional minutes wouldn't be catastrophic.

When Marlon's name was finally called, there was a thunderous roar from the crowd. Four family members were down in front taking pictures. A gift-wrapped box was given to him as he received his diploma. Mrs. Sanders, one of the teachers, had to usher Marlon down the stage because his posing for pictures was blocking the way for the next graduate. Marlon went back to his seat and thought with a grin, "I did it!" He was now a high school graduate. He had the diploma in one hand and a gift in the other to prove it. Twenty-six people in the audience were cheering for him. His Lincoln stretch was waiting outside for him. He had the world on the tip of his fingers, and his future before him. Marlon was so happy, he spent the rest of the program in a daze.

Afterwards, as he and the other graduates were removing their robes, they began to realize this might be the last time that they were going to see each other. Some were going to college; others to the military; and some were going to look for employment. Marlon was so happy that he had graduated from high school that neither he nor his family had thought about what he would do after graduation; he had plenty of time during the summer to figure that out. Many of the students said that they would stay in touch; maybe they'd have an annual picnic. After many hugs and tears, Marlon ran out of the auditorium to spend the rest of the night with his family. They had dinner reservations for 26 people at one of the finest restaurants in town, and they were driving there in the limousine. The restaurant was primarily frequented by Middle-class Whites and Blacks. Marlon enjoyed the ambience of the restaurant, and said as much to his family. "This is the kind of lifestyle that I want for the rest of my life," he said. Marlon couldn't remember the last time he had had so much fun.

Later that night, Mrs. Taylor walked into Marlon's room. Marlon was lying down on his back. His mother kissed him on the cheek and said, "I am very proud of you, my son." And Marlon said, "Thank you, Mom. Thanks for being there all the times that I needed you."

The morning after, however, is when reality began to set in. Marlon stared at his diploma and began wondering what was he going to do with the rest of his life. He asked himself, What is this piece of paper hanging up on my wall? Am I now an honorary citizen of the city? Will this diploma give me a job, or a business, so that I can take care of my family? Marlon wondered why today felt so different from yesterday. He wished that yesterday had never ended. He thought about all of his friends who entered high school with him as freshmen. Some of them were dead now, others were in jail, some were hanging on corners selling drugs, others were working as stock clerks, a few were working at fast-food chains. Would his future be any different from theirs? His associates, not friends had wanted him to drop out of school, but he always knew that he was going to finish. He had promised his mother. His mother had promised that if he did, she would give him a special night he would never forget. Now he doesn't want to forget it; he wants it to return; but it is no longer Sunday evening. It is now Monday morning for an eighteen-year-old African American male with a high school diploma and nowhere to go.

There are thousands of Marlons around the country. There are thousands of African American males who are not incarcerated, who graduated from high school but have no future. For a myriad of reasons, college was not their first choice after graduation. For many, they needed to be convinced that there was an economic payoff to education. Many African American males decide to try out their high school diploma on the job market before investing in college. Many African American males know that due to white male supremacy, a White male with a high school diploma will earn more than anyone else in America with a college degree. Most African American males are tired of a curriculum that is based on inaccurate information and irrelevant materials that are not applicable to their neighborhoods. Many are still wondering whether Columbus really did discover America. Did Abraham Lincoln really free the slaves? Regardless of whether it is true or not, what difference does it make if you live in the inner-city of America?

It is common knowledge that the government prefers to pay for inmates rather than college students. The joke on the streets is "commit a crime, go to jail, and while in jail, secure a college degree at the government's expense." A Black man has a much greater chance of getting an education in prison than from most American universities. Many African American males know that their GPA and test scores are not high enough for acceptance. Later in the week, Marlon began to write down the names of as many brothers that he could remember who had begun high school with him four years ago. Then he wrote down the names of the 75 brothers who had graduated with him and exactly what they were doing.

Of the 75 dropouts:

10 had died
15 were in prison
20 were selling drugs
12 were working in fast-food chains
18 were either underemployed, working off and on, laid-off, or in-between jobs.

Of the 75 graduates:

30 were in the military
20 went to college
25 were underemployed/unemployed/daydreaming.

Marlon laughed when he realized that he too was daydreaming.

What does America expect African American males to do after graduation? Germany and Japan have excellent apprentice programs. The governments of these two countries realize that there will always be a portion of their population that will not attend college, but as these people are very important to their economy, so they have worked with corporations to develop apprentice and internship programs for high school graduates. These programs increase the incentive to graduate from high school, because students have great confidence in their economic viability. The American system seems to be all or nothing, college, minimum wage, or welfare. It is true that in spite of the comparisons between American and Japanese educational systems K-12, the American college system is considered the best in the world. Witness the large numbers of immigrants that secure visas to complete their college studies in America. For those high school graduates who choose for a multiplicity of reasons not to attend college, a large number of them being African American, 66 percent females, 74 percent males,[1] what will African Americans do after graduation?

Does America expect African American males to go to a junior or community college? If they attended or graduated from a junior or community college, could America guarantee them a job? Or is the objective to enroll in a junior or community college and then pursue a degree from a four-year university? Does America provide more financial aid for students after they secure their A.A. degree than after their high school diploma? Does America want African American male high school graduates to become legal entrepreneurs? Are there programs in African American communities to identify capital and provide technical assistance for the development of business plans? Does the American public school system prepare African Americans for entrepreneurship? Is the American public school curriculum designed for employees or employers? Does America need African Americans to apply at U.S. Steel, General Motors, and Goodyear Rubber? Does America want African American males to relocate to Mexico and South Korea to work in plants for $.75 to $2.38 an hour? Does America want African American males to work in fast-food chains or clean hotels and other large corporate offices?

The daughters of a friend of mine who had relocated from Los Angeles to Atlanta were amazed and pleased when they saw large numbers of African Americans working in so many different occupations, that is, at restaurants, stores, and hotels. In Los Angeles, the Latino population, many of whom were in the country illegally, worked those jobs, and American corporations were paying them below minimum wage. Most African Americans refused to work at those jobs. Does America want African American male graduates to work for $2.00 an hour? Does America want African American male high school graduates to wash dishes, clean cars, and pump gas? Those jobs have been replaced by high-technology, which includes microchips and robots. Every time my car is washed at one of those automatic car washes, I still see Richard Pryor and seven other brothers who were working at the car wash. These eight men were able to visit eight young ladies after work, take them out on their meager wages, and with her salary consider marriage and a family. When I go through the car wash now, I wonder, where are those eight brothers? As much as I appreciate advances in technology, I'm still not convinced from an Africentric and a humanitarian perspective that it is the most productive way to empower 250 million Americans. Is it progress when a factory that once employed 1,000 people now, with robots and other computer-operated machines, only employs 100? I am not convinced that America has produced economic options for the nine hundred "downsized" employees (Ujamaa vs. capitalism). Ujamaa (cooperative economics) is very much in conflict with capitalism: capitalism is concerned with increasing profits; Ujamaa is concerned about the 900 people who were laid off.

The error in capitalism is this, however: when a company replaces the 900 people with a robot, while it has reduced its cost, it has not empowered the people to buy its products. Robots don't buy products -- people do. Downsizing inevitably forces American corporations to find new markets for their products.

Does America want African Americans to stand on corners? There are loitering laws now in some cities where if two or three people are gathered on a corner, they are subject to a fine or arrest. Does America want African Americans to make babies and stay home with their children and receive welfare? Historically, welfare laws were designed to discourage males from staying at home. Does America want African American males to join gangs, sell drugs, and kill each other with guns?

Marlon wants to know what America wants him to do with the rest of his life. What is America going to do with African American males with high school diplomas? Does America have a need for African American males with high school diplomas? Does America have a need for African American males without a diploma? Does America have a need for African American males with college or graduate degrees? I remember watching Minister Farrakhan on the *Donahue* show several years ago. Someone mentioned the 700,000 African American males in penal institutions and the $18,000-$38,000 that America spends annually, depending on the state, to incarcerate these brothers. This money comes primarily from middle-class taxpayers. Minister Farrakhan looked out at the audience and said, "You know our track record. You know what Elijah Muhammad did with Malcolm. You know what we can do with these brothers. We can turn an addict into a minister, a criminal into a security officer in a housing development center. We can turn a brother that has never worked into a brother that will sell one thousand newspapers, five hundred bean pies, and two hundred pounds of fish a week." He looked out to the audience and said, "White America, why don't you give them to us? You don't want them. You don't know what to do with them. You are spending billions of dollars to incarcerate them." Then he smiled and said, "And all we want are a couple of states."

America doesn't mind sending African American males to boot camp programs, but why won't America give these brothers to Minister Farrakhan and the Nation of Islam? If the objective is to balance the budget, wouldn't it be cheaper to give him Georgia or Alabama than to warehouse these brothers? What benefit does America gain in paying $18,000-$38,000 per person for 1,500,000 African Americans, not to mention the incalculable cost in the wasted productivity of the Marlon Taylors who are lying in bed or standing on corners wondering what to do with the rest of their lives? Could the answer be that the prison industry has become so financially lucrative that the private sector also wants a portion of the profits?

Entropy and the Black Man's Predicament

In physics the term "entropy" refers to energy, its unavailability for work, and the subsequent disorder and chaos that state produces. When a system is void of its essential maintenance resource, i.e., energy, it is deprived of the capacity to carry out its ascribed function. At this juncture the system begins to disintegrate randomly and becomes a hostile force, arbitrarily, capriciously, and spontaneously bombarding other units, quite often causing damage and death to these units before ultimately succumbing itself. When I first learned of this term, I immediately saw the parallels between physics and technology and sociology. If any part in a machine cannot achieve its purpose, then it will wreak havoc upon all other parts surrounding it.

And so it goes with humans. Every human has a purpose. If a human is unable to achieve his purpose, then he too will wreak havoc upon all the other people around him. Man's primary purpose is to economically provide and protect his family. If men are not allowed to provide for their family economically, then they will begin to destroy all the other men around them while simultaneously causing damage to themselves.

What does America expect of the 75 members of Marlon's freshman class who did not graduate? What does America expect for them to do? What does America expect Marlon to do if he chooses not to go to college or the military, and internship and apprentice programs are unavailable? Can a man be a man in America without income? Can an unemployed man be a man in a patriarchal, capitalistic, materialistic economy? Woman's primary role is to give birth and nurture children. This remains viable and feasible for women.

The assumption that crime is based on need implies that the poorest people in America should be more actively involved in crime. If that was the case, then Black women should be committing crimes in greater numbers than anyone else. The reality is, there are more than 700,000 African American males in prison, while there are less than 70,000 African American women - or 10 percent of that total. The myth that crime is based on need is easily dispelled with the reality that 80 percent of the crime in America is white collar crime -- computer embezzlement and savings and loan scandals. A White male stockbroker embezzles $6,000,000 and receives a $5,500 fine. An unemployed Black male steals a TV set and receives six years in jail. Crime is not based on need; crime is based on greed or power. African American men want the same power White men have. It is an unfortunate relationship in America that for every one percent increase in male unemployment there is a 4.3 percent increase in wife abuse. Why should these two factors, male unemployment and wife abuse, be correlated? The reverse is not true. Every one percent increase in female unemployment does not precipitate an increase in male abuse. It is obvious that the genders operate on two different value systems.

My wife and I were watching TV news accounts of the horrors in Rwanda. Although the media refused to place the conflict in a historical context, we understood that European imperialism had divided the country into two warring factions and placed handpicked puppets in power. At one point in the story, the commentator interviewed an African woman. She, her husband, and their seven children had walked more than one hundred miles from Rwanda to the Zaire border. In this very hilly terrain where very little grows, she was trying to settle her family for the evening. The commentator wanted to know why her husband was simply sitting next to the tree. My wife also wanted to know, because you see the same behavior pattern among many African American men. She wanted to know what is it about African manhood that allows a man to sit still when there's work to be done. I asked a brother from Liberia for his opinion. He said it was about pride. In the past, African men were able to provide for their families, economically, but when that was taken from them, it effected their psyche. For many, unemployment paralyzes; they seem unable to do whatever it takes to feed and clothe their children. In the United States you see the same pattern. Say there's a man and a woman both working menial jobs. They are both subject to verbal abuse from White supervisors. The woman endures because she has mouths to feed at home, but many brothers get frustrated and walk away. While I understand the issue of power, pride and ego; while I understand that in Los Angeles African Americans resent (now) being on the same level as immigrants who just crossed the border and speak no English, while I understand that many of these businesses are taking advantage of the immigrants and paying them less than minimum wage, I still believe that some income is better than no income. Legal work is better than illegal work. There is pride to be found in a good day's work. This may be the most pivotal issue men have to resolve.

In our crime watch group, we had a long discussion about those in our race who were so frustrated with the lack of economic options that they would choose to either not work or to work illegally. Many older African American men don't understand the issues facing younger African American males. Many of these older men still remember the good old days when they arrived in the industrial belt in the forties and fifties and jobs were plentiful. You could drop out of school at 16, or 18 if you were like Marlon and had graduated, and earn between $8 and $18 an hour. With very little education, these men were able to provide a middle-class lifestyle for their families. When they retired, however, their job and that $18 per hour were not bequeathed to their sons. Corporations either closed the plant and opened one overseas, or hired part-time workers to avoid paying medical benefits. Unfortunately, the ideology and memory of many older African American men are irreconcilable with the present economy. This older population has a tremendous communication problem with younger African American males. I often remind these older brothers of the Sheraton Hotel story in Chicago. A rumor was released that the Sheraton would be hiring 5,000 people the following morning. The following morning there were some 10,000-15,000 African Americans, large numbers of them men, looking for any type of job, and waiting outside in 17°-below-0 weather. I don't know if those older brothers did that in the 1940s.

Within the context of this term - entropy - it has been said that a man's most productive economic years will be the following twenty years after formal education. As Marlon lies in bed looking up at the ceiling wondering about his options, the theory says that his most productive economic years will be between eighteen and thirty-eight. For his classmates who dropped out of school before receiving their diploma, let's say at sixteen, their most productive years will be between sixteen and thirty-six. For African American males between the ages of sixteen and thirty-six, or between eighteen and thirty-eight, this is the time of entropy. Since there are no jobs at which to expend energy, then the men will be dangerous to themselves and those around him. This is the time of entropy when they are most dangerous, not only to themselves (suicide), but to other people (homicide).

When high school principals give me the opportunity to speak just to their male students, I am humbled to speak to 500-1000 African American males between fourteen and nineteen years of age. I look at them, I see their potential, and I imagine what would happen if these 1000 brothers could be converted to the liberation struggle and join organizations that give our community direction. It is also a frustrating experience to speak to these young brothers and know statistically where they'll be 20 years from now. One-tenth will be dead, via homicide, suicide, or some type of accident. One-third will be either using or dealing drugs. One-fourth will be in prison. Others will be marginally employed. I ask the Lord to allow them to see Him when they see me and to allow me to give the best speech of my life.

Realistically, though, even if I make the best speech my words will go in one ear and out the other if there is no follow-up. I remember when one principal brought in 100 men to talk to the boys in small groups after my speech. That made the program more significant, because there was a follow-up, but that was just one day. These boys need attention each and every day.

I have a fantasy that after a speech, buses would take these thousand African American males from their urban environment and take them to the country. We would keep them safe and teach them Africentric manhood. We'd send them back when they turned 30 years old, when they have mellowed out. When they are no longer dangerous. When they know "whose" they are, "who" they are, who the enemy is and empowerment strategies.

In his book *Black on Black Violence*, Amos Wilson points out a significant difference between Black and White male suicides. Black men kill themselves with their futures ahead of them, White men with their futures behind them. "One dies blossoming in the Spring; the other after the first frost of Autumn. The Black man has packed all the guilt, failure, shame, fatalism, pain, hopelessness, and cynicism of a lifetime within a life span of three decades. Somehow the cavalier optimism of youth and willful self-confidence of young manhood are dissipated at or before the point of actualization and assumptions of their powers to transform the world. Somehow Black youth and young adults are born into and come early to exist in a different ominous reality: one that was created for them; one under the control of others."[2]

That created "reality" negates, diminishes, and saps the will to live. Life seems pointless, an absurdity filled with bitter irony, a happenstance, a quicksand where every effort at self-rescue only seems to pull one under more rapidly and where every branch thrown to a sinking man breaks as he struggles to reach safe ground. Remember in entropy, not only does the useless unit wreak havoc upon the other surrounding units, but also to itself. Thus it becomes very difficult to distinguish Black homicide from Black suicide, which we will discuss in chapter four in more detail.

So Marlon sits in his room trying to reconcile his Sunday night experience with his Monday morning reality. He played the game the way it was supposed to be played. He stayed in school, eight years in elementary, four years in high school, but where is the pot of gold at the end of the rainbow? Some African American males have played the game an additional four years in college, and they are still looking for the pot of gold. Conformity is sold to White Americans, and for the most part, it works for them. White Americans are convinced that if you follow the rules, you can live the American Dream. African American males want the American Dream too; unfortunately, many are trying to achieve it by refusing to conform to the rules. As youth, we used to believe that if you secured a good education and worked hard there would be an economic windfall at the end. Today our youth believe that nonconformity may be a better option. They have seen too many Marlons with high school diplomas with nothing else to do but hang out on corners. They've seen too many brothers with college degrees who are still looking for employment. Many African Americans, especially African American males, now believe that the path to the American Dream is not education and hard work, but a sports or rap contract, or worse, a drug deal.

Marlon's White counterpart across town also celebrated graduation Sunday. Ironically, he too will sell drugs, but his drugs will be legal. He will work for a pharmaceutical company, and he will be paid a base salary and commissions. I often see these young men on airplanes. These White males who neither finished, nor in some cases, attend college, will make more than most African Americans with college degrees. Those White males who graduated from high-school on Sunday night will now tell my mother and father what to do on Monday morning, as they become vice-presidents of their daddys' firms. If only African American males had a legal product to sell. Black men who have gotten caught up in the drug trade obviously have the tenacity and an expertise in selling. Many of these drug dealers work 10-24 hours a day. They understand advertising, math, and accounting. They promote their product by giving it to you free to see if you like it. They can convert kilos to grams to dollar bills without the use of a calculator. They are masters at collecting outstanding debts. Any corporation could utilize those types of skills, if only these brothers had a legal product to sell. I commend Minister Farrakhan, Father Pfleger, and others who have given young brothers legal products to sell.

Have we as adults given up on these young brothers? Lately I've been hearing too many of us say that since we can't save the 14-19-year-olds, we should concentrate our efforts on the younger children. I have heard and understand the statement. I am a strong advocate of prevention, that is, correcting the problem before it develops and grows. I understand the Fourth Grade Syndrome and I advocate correcting problematic behavior in Black male children before they get to the fourth grade. Intervention at fourth grade is more cost-effective than at twelfth grade. Given the need for prevention and early intervention I still must ask the question, Are we giving up on Black male teens because it is the most feasible option? Or are we incapacitated and impotent? Are we giving up because we have limited human and financial resources? Are we doubting God's ability to save these brothers between 14 and 19 years of age? Do we as adults feel so weak and helpless? Are the problems so acute and grave? If African American adults don't save these young men, who is going to save them?

If we decide to save the youth between nine and thirteen years of age, what are we going to do with them when they become fourteen? Do we stay with this young group until they become adults? Or do we abandon them to negative peer pressure, gangster rap, gang bangers, drug dealers, and a hostile media? Do we take them to the countryside and bring them back to the city when they're thirty? How do you think we'll be able to sell our program to the younger ones if we aren't able to sell it to the teens?

W.E.B. Du Bois, in the early 1900s stated that the major question of the twentieth century was going to be the color question. Clearly, he has been proven correct, and I believe racism will continue into the twenty-first century. In addition, I believe that economics will assume equal prominence in the twenty-first century quest for African American parity. Specifically, the question for the Black middle class and Du Bois' Talented Tenth will be, How many people do you employ? Maybe the reason why African American adults *sell* their future is because they don't *employ* their future.

The reason for the Nation of Islam's success is that when they go into prisons they go in with more than ideas: they provide basic goods and services. They provide suits, newspapers, bean pies, and security contracts. Amil Cabral taught that intellectuals discuss ideas, but the masses respond to basic goods and services. Are we as a race and a community going to succumb to entropy? Are we going to self-destruct? Does America really believe that African American males that suffer entropy are simply going to stay silent in the ghetto and slowly die? We need to read Claude Brown's *Man Child in the Promised Land*, Richard Wright's *Native Son*, Nathan McCall's *Make Me Want to Holler*. This chapter has looked at Marlon's economic options with a diploma. The next chapter will look at Jerome's chances for a college degree.

What will African American males do after high school graduation?

ℭHAPTER 𝒯HREE

The Black Male on Campus

African Americans hold the unfortunate distinction of being the only group in America to have more males in prison (1,500,000) than in college (600,000). African Americans are the only group in America in which females outnumber males (900,000 to 600,000) in college enrollment. Of the 1,500,000 African Americans in college, 20 percent, or 267,000, attend Black colleges. Black colleges enroll a mere 16 percent of the total Black student body, yet they graduate more than 37 percent; that percentage represented 41,012 females and 24,326 males. African American females comprised 61 percent of all African American students in college and 63 percent of African American graduates. Thirty-two percent of all African American female high school graduates attend college, in comparison to 26 percent of African American males. The overall retention rate for African American college students is 43 percent - 41 percent for females, 53 percent for female athletes, 33 percent for males, and 43 percent for male athletes.[1]

Listed below are the fifty colleges and universities that produced the largest number of African American graduates;

RANK	INSTITUTION	STATE	MEN	WOMEN	TOTAL	%Grad	%Ret
1	Howard University	DC	415	673	1088	78.6	46
2	Hampton University	VA	257	572	829	97.8	85
3	Southern Univ. - (Baton Rouge)	LA	280	445	725	92.5	25
4	N. Carolina Agricultural & Tech	NC	293	373	666	88.8	38
5	Grambling State University	LA	207	341	548	95.1	45
6	Jackson State University	MS	202	326	528	95.8	34

7	Wayne State University	M I	149	373	522	16.5	53
8	Univ. of the Dist. of Columbia	DC	225	272	497	87.8	34
9	FL Agric. & Mech. University	F L	146	317	463	79.0	33
10	North Carolina Central Univ.	NC	138	324	462	91.3	82
11	South Carolina State College	S C	179	280	459	92.2	52
12	Morgan State University	MD	158	299	457	92.0	16
13	Norfolk State University	V A	134	311	445	93.0	55
14	Chicago State University	I L	114	323	437	86.9	7
15	Univ. of Maryland College Park	MD	184	238	422	7.7	45
16	Prairie View A & M University	T X	190	231	421	79.7	25
17	Temple University	PA	113	274	387	11.1	24
18	Spelman College	GA	0	376	376	98.2	--
19	CUNY City College	NY	167	199	366	29.3	--
20	Rutgers Univ. New Brunswick	N J	124	240	364	7.1	59
21	Tennessee State University	T N	132	227	359	69.6	39
22	Tuskegee University	A L	150	207	357	94.7	70
23	Southern IL Univ.-Carbondale	I L	203	142	345	7.5	5
24	Texas Southern University	T X	104	239	343	66.7	9
25	College of New Rochelle	NY	55	142	326	56.7	67
26	Virginia State University	V A	150	239	325	91.3	64
27	Morehouse College	G A	317	271	317	96.9	84
28	Univ. of S. Carolina at Columbia	S C	94	185	315	10.3	55
29	Bethune Cookman College	F L	87	0	306	93.9	34
30	CUNY Hunter College	NY	73	215	288	18.1	--
31	Memphis State University	T N	107	174	281	15.1	28
32	CUNY Bernard Baruch College	NY	98	180	278	16.1	--
33	Elizabeth City State University	NC	102	175	277	79.4	78
34	Winston-Salem State University	N C	89	188	277	83.7	68
35	Michigan State Univ.	M I	83	193	276	3.8	48
36	Alabama State Univ.	A L	93	182	275	79.9	N/A
37	N. Carolina St. Univ. at Raleigh	NC	115	160	275	8.1	40
38	Southern Univ. at New Orleans	L A	82	192	274	90.4	--
39	Univ. of California-Los Angeles	CA	100	173	273	5.2	54
40	Univ. of Arkansas-Pine Bluff	A R	90	176	266	85.3	--
41	Univ. of Maryland Univ. College	MD	105	161	266	15.4	--
42	University of Florida	F L	89	174	263	4.8	44
43	Xavier University	L A	70	192	262	84.2	--
44	Alcorn State University	MS	89	172	261	97.0	25
45	Univ. of California-Berkeley	CA	89	170	259	4.8	58
46	Univ. of N. Carolina at Chapel Hill	N C	87	165	252	7.1	59
47	Georgia State Univ.	GA	77	172	249	10.7	35
48	Alabama State Univ.	A L	77	169	246	97.6	16
49	Florida State Univ.	F L	84	160	244	5.0	39
50	Clark Atlanta Univ.	GA	70	172	242	98.4	80

Let's look at this data from an Africentric perspective. I mentioned earlier that 26 percent of Black male high school graduates are attending college. In most large urban areas the high school drop-out rate nears 50 percent. While I have seen figures saying that 80 percent of African American high school students graduate from high school, I don't trust school districts to follow the paper trail of students who have been expelled, pushed-out, transferred, etc. In a typical urban African American school, there are 200 entering freshmen. For this discussion, let's say that one hundred are male and one hundred are female. According to the 80 percent graduation rate statistic, 160 students, including 80 males, will graduate from high school four to five years later. What makes tracking difficult for schools is that some of those 200 students who entered as freshman will probably graduate elsewhere. Although it is difficult to determine actual graduation rates for African American males in urban high schools, the real numbers fall somewhere between 50 and 80 percent. For the sake of discussion, let's use the midway point of 65 percent. And since numbers don't give us the real story, it is at this point we want to become more personal and meet Jerome Brown, an African American freshman attending a predominantly Black high school in the inner-city.

In Jerome's freshman class there are 200 entering students, 100 male and 100 female. Four years later, the year of graduation, the class no longer has 200 students. With a 35 percent drop-out rate, or a 65 percent graduation rate, we lost 70 students, one of whom might be Jerome. Of the 70 students that we lost, using a ratio of two-thirds for the males and one-third for the females, because the male to female dropout rate is 2:1 we lost approximately 23 females and 47 males. Remember, we started out with 100 males and 100 females, but on graduation day we will have 53 males and 77 females. In simple math, there is a 50 percent chance that we will not see Jerome on graduation day.

Since this chapter is looking at African American

males in college, Jerome will be one of the fortunate males to graduate from high school. Of the 53 male graduates, remember, only 26 percent of that number will have the opportunity to attend college. Twenty-six percent of 53 equals a grand total of 14 male students of the 100 males who were high school freshman four years ago. On the other hand, 77 females will graduate from high school. Thirty-three percent, or 26, will attend college. Of the 14 African American males that went to college, with a college graduation rate of 33 percent, it means approximately five male students will graduate from college.

The odds are five percent in Jerome's favor that he will graduate from college. That is the grim reality facing African American males pursuing a college education. With those odds, you begin to at least understand why they believe they have a better chance of achieving the American Dream by selling drugs or securing a rap or NBA contract than getting a college degree. In the preceding chapter we discussed Marlon's economic options with a high school diploma. Jerome is also concerned about the economic viability of a college degree. Will Jerome be able to work in his major at a middle-income salary?

Isn't it interesting that, for both males and females, athletes have a higher graduation rate than regular students. The female athlete has a 12 percent greater chance of graduating from college than her nonathletic counterpart. Males have a 10 percent greater possibility. Although the stereotype of the "dumb jock" prevails, the reality is that athletes actually perform better, and there are many reasons why. For example African Americans on athletic scholarships have a more secure financial base, which allows them to focus more on their sport and their studies. There are a large number of athletes on scholarships majoring in Physical Education. I am not belittling its academic rigor, but in my opinion, it is not as challenging as a degree in premed, accounting, chemistry, or computer science.

Contrary to the belief that academic failure is the

major reason for African Americans dropping out of college, its the lack of financial resources. For some strange reason, students receiving financial aid receive less with each passing year. The financial package is based on the premise that with each passing year of college, the student will earn more income. Apparently the White establishment that designed this package was not aware of the vast numbers of African American college graduates who are unemployed. Why should we assume that a college sophomore will earn more then a freshman and a college junior will earn more then a sophomore and that a college senior will earn more then a college junior?

It is this faulty and incorrect assumption, that African Americans, will earn greater income with each passing year of college that contributes to a low retention rate. Unless African American parents own businesses or have excellent corporate connections, or unless students receive internships through programs like INROADS with Fortune 500 corporations, the search for employment will be difficult.

Another reason for the low graduation rate among African American students is that they often feel a sense of isolation, loneliness and a lack of belonging, especially in White schools. College athletes benefit from having a coach, often African American, who becomes a role model if not a mentor. Another major reason for the low retention rate is students' lack of discipline and time management skills. Many students who have additional responsibilities, e.g., athletics, employment, and other extracurricular activities, ironically improve their GPA because they learn to manage more wisely the little discretionary time they have.

The life of college athletes becomes more complex when Propositions 42, 48, 16, and 14 are thrown into the equation. Each proposition demands a higher GPA and test scores on achievement tests. Many African American coaches feel it is unfair to have higher standards for athletes than for regular students. Secondly, tests have not been the best barometer of college success, African American coaches want more weight placed on GPA rather than a biased test. African American coaches see athletic scholarships as an opportunity for African American males to attend college; without them, college would be financially impossible. College scholarships should not be denied them by the NCAA due to culturally bias over-weighted tests before they have the opportunity to demonstrate their academic acumen on the actual college curriculum.

On the other hand, the late Arthur Ashe, David Robinson, and other athletes take the opposing view that it is not very demanding of the NCAA to require athletes to have a 2.0 to a 2.2 GPA and a 16-18 on the ACT or 700-900 on the SAT. My major concern has been that the burden, as usual, is always placed on the victim, and we don't place pressure on high school teachers, elementary school teachers, and coaches. We expect the student athlete in the last two or three years of high school to eradicate ten years of miseducation. Coaches who value academics and infuse studies into their programs have been more effective. It is no accident that schools like the University of North Carolina, Georgetown, Penn State, Duke, Providence College, LaSalle University, Boston College, and Notre Dame graduate above 80 percent of the African American athletes, and some in the high 90s. In other schools, such as the University of Las Vegas, Texas at El Paso, Memphis State, the University of Louisville, Tennessee State, Texas Southern, Alabama State, and Prairie View, a mere 20 percent of athletes graduate. It is obvious that some schools will admit you and other schools will help you graduate.

I admire and respect John Thompson the former basketball coach at Georgetown. Georgetown invested $60,000 to house and educate Patrick Ewing for four years; the return on that investment was $12 million in TV contracts. John Thompson thought that the least Georgetown could do to support their star player was provide a five-year scholarship if necessary, tutorial service on the road, and a counselor to monitor his progress. It did not surprise me to see John Thompson advising his star of ten years ago during the NBA playoffs because of the bond that was nurtured back in college. Such personal attention is a major contributing factor to the high graduation of the male athlete.

When I talk to students like Jerome and his girlfriend Renee on a typical college campus and ask them what the ratio is between females and males on their college campus, they'll tell me it's two to one. Many will say three to one, four to one, or five to one. Actually, there are 818,000 African American females, or 61 percent, and 517,000 African American males, or 39 percent. This is a 1.5 to 1.0 ratio, not three, four, five, or six to one. If we look at the graduation ratio, African American females do move from 60 percent up to 63 percent of the graduates, and African American males drop from 40 percent to 37 percent. The graduation rate is 41 percent for African American females, 33 percent for African American males - an eight-point differential. Yet when I ask people about the graduation figures, you get the impression that the figures multiply exponentially. Why is there a difference between perception and statistical reality? For one reason, sisters often forget about the athletes, many of whom are seldom seen at cultural activities. They may not attend because of their schedules and or their lack of political consciousness. Also, if brothers are involved with White women or women of other ethnic groups, oftentimes sisters will dismiss them from the population. Of course, these variables are possible for females as well, but they're not as affected by athletics, political apathy, and interracial dating as are African American males.

Sisters often ignore brothers who are studious. They are often accused of acting White because they choose to be in the library instead of someone's dormitory room; thus they may also be eliminated from the population. If you refer to the table of the fifty colleges and universities that produced the most African American graduates (pgs. 33 and 34), you'll see not one school with more male graduates than female. This excludes, of course, Morehouse College, which does not admit females. 1990 was the first year in which North Carolina A&T had a greater number of female graduates, there were 373 African American female graduates to 293 African American males. A major reason why North Carolina A&T historically had a larger number of male graduates than female is that the academic emphasis was in engineering. African American males have fared better in universities like Tuskegee and Prairie View, which concentrate in engineering.

Why does Jerome and other African American males have a lower retention rate than their girlfriends? The retention rate is 41 percent for African American females, 33 percent for African American males. I won't even fathom what the retention for African American males would be if it were not for a 10 percent higher retention rate for the African American male athlete and the disproportionate number of African American male students who receive athletic scholarships. The retention rate could plunge to 20 percent if we excluded African American male athletes.

The following questions should stimulate discussion and thought around the African American male/female retention disparity:

✓ Do males experience greater institutional racism in college than females?

✓ Do males experience more racism at Black colleges?

✓ Do females possess greater discipline than males? If so, why?

✓ Do females manage their time better than males? If so, why?

✓ Do females have more African American role models on campus than males?

✓ Do females complete their assignments more often than males? If so, why?

✓ Are females more computer literate? If so, why?

✓ Do females utilize the concept of cooperative learning more effectively than males? If so, why?

✓ Are males more distracted academically by their social life than females? If so, why?

✓ Are males more distracted by their dating habits, which may include more than one female at a time?

✓ Are females more focused, driven, and goal-oriented than males? If so, why?

✓ Do more males than females feel that returning home to their mothers is a viable option? If so, why?

✓ Do females attend class more often than males? If so, why?

✓ Do females study more than males? If so, why?

✓ Do males cram more than females? If so, why?

✓ Are males more affected by negative peer pressure than females? If so, why?

✓ Do males spend more time listening to music than females? If so, why?

✓ Are males more emotionally involved in pledging than females? If so, why?

✓ Are males more involved in the liberation struggle and Black student union activities than females? If so, why?

✓ Could the difference in retention have something to do with the dynamic of some mothers raising their daughters and loving their sons?

✓ Do males spend more time getting high than females?

✓ Do males, excluding those on varsity teams, engage in more sports or get involved in more athletic activities than females?

✓ Are males more affected by car ownership than females?

✓ Do males spend more time traveling visiting friends at other colleges than females?

✓ Are males more interested in the option of earning money in illegal ways than females, e.g., selling drugs?

Which of the above behaviors are affected by external factors like racism, and which by internal factors like responsibility, discipline, laziness, and apathy? Can racism be responsible for African American males not attending class? Or spending more time with their frat than with their books? How about the brother who's trying to figure out how he can date three sisters at the same time when he should be completing his ten-page paper in biology? Is the White man responsible for that? How did the White man make African American men drink and snort more than African American women?

Please remember, I am the author of *Countering the Conspiracy to Destroy Black Boys*. I definitely know a conspiracy when I see one. I am very much aware that it is not an accident that every President in this country has been a White male and that Black median income is only 61 percent of White median income. If you live in a world controlled by White men, then their greatest threat is Black men not Black women. The best way to destroy the Black family is to destroy the Black man.

However you want to label it - conspiracy, happenstance, a strange occurrence - I definitely believe there is something unfair and unjust about the disproportionate number of African American males who are placed in special ed, remedial reading, and suspension from K-12. This lays the groundwork for what happens to them in college. In her book *Blacks in College*, Jacqueline Fleming points out that African American males perform better at Black colleges than they do at White colleges, primarily because they feel confident about securing leadership positions. And while she discovered that both Black males and females suffer from being in hostile campus environments, males seem to be more adversely affected.

> Since black, as well as white males are similarly deprived, they are predisposed to interact competitively. The racial difference serves to intensify the basically hostile nature of male-male interactions. Black males have been excluded from participation in a wide range of activities and restricted to small groups of all black social and political organizations. Apparently, the restricted role that black males play, both within the classroom and without, acts to constrict intellectual gains that issue from being an actor in campus goings on. Upon entering what is in some sense alien territory, black males fall into the category of sub-dominate males by virtue of their visibility and small numbers. Interestingly, observers of primate animal hierarchies find that sub-dominate males lapse into a non-confrontational, lethargic state of behavior that can only be described as depression. In many ways the developmental profiles of black males in white colleges also can be described as depressed. They become unhappy with

college life, they feel that they have been treated unfairly, they display academic de-motivation and think less of their abilities. They profess losses of energy and cease to be able to enjoy competitive activities. To be sure, there are ways in which these males do act depressed in as much as they become assertive and they participate energetically in certain campus activities. Nonetheless, these developments are defensive and do little to remedy their plight. Black men often try to work the problem out through their interpersonal lives. They may try to attach dominance over women or live through children. In black colleges, which offer so many opportunities for social ascendence, these interpersonal strains can be ignored.

If Black women suppress their assertive selves to please men, then we can understand why it is easier for them to develop their assertive abilities on white campuses. The data indicates that on most predominately white college campuses there are few black men, especially among seniors. Furthermore, we know that on predominately white campuses black males are often undergoing depressive reactions that cause them to withdraw academically and psychologically. In other words, they are not men enjoying dominance, social ascendence or their own assertive abilities. In this context black women may very well be able to develop their assertive capacities that help them hold their own intellectually.[3]

I remember when I first entered college. There were 1,000 African American freshman; four years later only 254 of us graduated. I knew that we did not graduate because we were smarter; we were disciplined, managed our time well, studied often, attended class, avoided cramming, studied together, and utilized tutors. If you look at the 606,000 African American males in college and the retention rate of 33 percent, that means there are 400,000 African American males who are not going to graduate. I wonder, Will they ever go back to college? Will they ever achieve their goals? What is the state of their psyche? At what level is their self-esteem?

It was difficult getting Jerome from high school into college. I worry whether Jerome will be in the category of 341,000 that did not graduate or the 170,000 that did. I don't like what I see when I witness Black male failure. Whenever I speak in small southern towns, inevitably my host will drive by a corner and point out the African American males who used to be star athletes. They were this close to receiving a million dollar contract; now they are busboys in restaurants and still talking trash on the corner about how they were one step away from becoming a multi-millionaire. I am concerned about African American males who drop out of college for financial reasons and end up working at menial jobs.

My parents both worked for the post office. There they observed numerous college students who often quit school because the money was good. For that reason, my parents did not allow me to work there. Langston Hughes raises the question in his poem, "What happens to a dream deferred?" When I ask African American students about their majors, invariably they'll tell me business, computer science, communications, criminal justice, and accounting. The African American community has so many problems that all majors are welcome and necessary. I also ask them did you choose your major based on your interests, the community, or what is more financially lucrative. Unfortunately, there are very few African Americans, specifically males, majoring in education. African American children comprise 17 percent of the children in public schools nationwide, but only 1.2 percent are African American males. There are several states and more than twenty colleges that grant special scholarships to African American males who will agree to teach for several years.

The next chapter will discuss why Marlon and Jerome's associates are killing each other.

Why Do Black Men Kill Black Men?

*C*HAPTER *F*OUR

Why Do Black Men Kill Black Men?

"The Lord will let the people be governed by immature boys. Everyone will take advantage of everyone
else. Young people will not respect their elders. And
worthless people will not respect their superiors." Isaiah
3: 4-5, from the Good News Bible.

W hen you read that scripture you wonder if
you are reading today's newspaper rather
than something written two thousand years
ago. Communities are now controlled by
boys, and young people do not respect their elders. This
is the first generation of African Americans that does not
respect their elders. It is the first generation of elders who
are afraid of their children. Parents are afraid of their children. Parents say, "We do not know what to do with him."
There are housing developments with 20,000 people that
were designed for 5,000. Of the 20,000 people, approximately 15,000 are children. Of the five thousand adults,
4,500 or more are women. There are housing developments where there are few if any men. Men used to
supervise our parks, so that if two boys got into a fight, at
least one man would be there to break it up. A park today
may have 300 children present and not one man available
to supervise. Immature boys now distribute justice and
determine right from wrong and decide who may have to
pay with their lives.

In Baltimore, like so many cities with ethnic enclaves,
there is a neighborhood called Little Italy. On the other
side of the street is the African American community,
sometimes called a ghetto. Little Italy is a working-class

neighborhood, with manicured lawns, and populated by Italians. There is very little crime in Little Italy. If there is an act of violence in Little Italy, it becomes a newsworthy event. The media will often find out about crime in Little Italy after the men there have already resolved it. Please note, I said *the men* of Little Italy, not the police of Baltimore. Little Italy has very little crime, not because of extra police who walk the streets, not because of an incestuous relationship with City Hall, but because Italian men have taught Italian boys the importance of community. They are taught early on what behaviors are allowed and not allowed to take place there. In Little Italy it is not surprising to see women, including elderly women, walking the streets by themselves late at night and not be bothered, except for the occasional, "Would you like an escort home?"

Across the street in the African American neighborhood, however, anything and everything is allowed to take place there and only the bizarre is reported by the media. If someone is shot, the media will probably ignore it because shootings happen daily. The media may become interested if three to five people are shot or if a White person or some significant African American official was accosted there. As for the indigenous residents, their problems will probably go unreported.

If a Black woman was walking down the street late at night by herself and someone was walking toward her, she would probably hope that the person walking toward her be a Black woman first, a White woman second, a White male third and the Black male last. Black men send fear in the hearts of Black women. The Italian woman in Little Italy would hope to see an Italian man, *first*, an Italian woman second, a Black woman third, and the Black male never. An Italian woman in Little Italy desires an Italian man first; a Black woman in the Black community desires a Black man last. I believe when African American women will prefer African American men first our liberation from white supremacy will be achieved.

Why do you think Little Italy is different from the Black community? Little Italy could also be Little Chinatown, Little Korea, or Little Arabia. It is unfair to compare a community of immigrants who voluntarily came to America with their culture intact to a people that were forced to come and had their culture stolen. Culture is very important; it is your racial DNA. It gives you a sense of history, a blueprint for living, and direction for the future. Culture is far more than food, dress, and music. Culture is synonymous with lifestyle, values, history, purpose, and direction. A people without their culture are a people without a past, present, and future. A people without their culture do not know how to live. A people without their culture are no longer a people and they will act like animals. A people without their culture will be afraid of each other and won't trust each other. They will not pool their resources to start their own businesses or to support those that exist. A people without their culture will be afraid to walk down the street at three o'clock in the morning and meet someone who looks like them because they can never be sure whether they share a value system. A people without a culture and values are dangerous.

Little Italy, Little Chinatown, Little Korea, and Little Arabia are different, not because they receive additional police support but because they have an intact culture. Their culture drives them to become economically self-sufficient and teaches their boys and girls rites of passage.

Two excellent books that describe life in those African American communities where culture is often nonexistent are *Do or Die* by Leon Bing and *Monster: The Autobiography of a L.A. Gang Member* by "Monster" Cody Scott (Sanyika Shakur). Says Shakur, "If I had been born in '53 instead of '63, I would have been a Black Panther. If I had born in Germany in the early '30s, I would have probably joined the Nationalist Socialist Party. If I had been born Jewish, I would have joined the Jewish Defense League because I have the energy, the vitality to be part of something with power, either constructive or destructive. And because there was a destructive element around me when I was growing up, I went into the Crypts."[1]

I have noticed that wherever I go in the world - New York, Chicago, L.A, Toronto, Haiti, Jamaica, London, Botswana, Egypt, or Ghana - African men love to stand on corners. I have often wondered why brothers love hanging out on corners. Are they waiting for their picture to be taken? Do they want people to see them? What is it they want people to see? Are they afraid that they are going to miss something if they are inside and not on the corner? What do they expect to see? Who drives by those corners? Shakur suggests that there's something about the nighttime that make corners more exciting; and we control the night. Cody Scott described how important it was being in a gang. He compared shooting someone with an orgasm; that it was a sense of power. That my gun became the great equalizer.[2]

In my research, I have found that 95 percent of the boys in jail were on the corners between ten o'clock at night and three o'clock in the morning, and that is why I tell parents, If you can't control any other time, control between 10:00pm and 3:00am. Once you know the time and the place, you have increased your chances for victory. We know the place is the corner, and we know the time is 10:00pm-3:00am. We also need to understand the root reasons why African men hang out on the corner. Why do more African men hang out on corners than African women? Why do corners provide greater excitement, intrigue, and mystique for men than women? Shakur's favorite phrase was "putting work in for the gang." His choice of words was very similar to my father who always said he was putting in work at the post office. I knew that meant 8-10 hours a day, and Shakur meant the same thing with the Crypts. Gangbanging became a full-time job, and his shift started at 8:00pm and ended at 4:00am.

The corner becomes more important if it becomes an issue of turf. If there are two rival forces in the area, they will behave just like countries that are involved in military combat; each group feels they must protect their turf. Add drugs to the equation, and turf becomes a distribution center. Coca Cola, Pepsi or any other corporation also goes to great lengths to protect their distribution system. While in past generations, young males grew up, left the gang, and secured a job, today brothers are hanging out on corners longer because jobs are unavailable. While mothers would prefer their sons to play outside, for many African American males life has to be lived inside. If life has to be lived in seclusion, if men can't walk down the street as they do in Little Italy, then what point is life?

I am also grappling with the question, Why do Black men kill Black men? Why don't they kill White men? Why do Black men kill Black men more than Black women kill Black women? Why don't Black men protect Black women? Why don't they protect Black children? Why don't they protect Black elders? Why don't Black males protect their turf from foreign businesses? Could the reason why African American men don't protect Black women, their elders, or Black children be because they have not been taught to do that? Could the reason why Black men don't keep foreign businesses out of their neighborhood be because they have not been taught to do that? Could the reason why Black men do not kill White people be because they have not been taught to do that? Could the reason why Black men kill Black men be because that is what they have been taught to do? Nathan McCall writes in *Makes Me Wanna Holler* that he received thirty days in jail for almost killing a Black man, but received twelve years in jail for robbing a White store; there were no injuries. Had he been taught something? Had he been taught to devalue Black male life that day? There is a powerful scene in the movie *Juice* between Tupac and his adversary. Tupac is on the run and tells his adversary that he himself isn't _ h _ _, and that if he himself isn't _ h _ _ then the adversary ain't _ h _ _. He was saying, if I hate myself, you know what I think of you.

Amos Wilson brilliantly captures the Black man's sense of self-loathing in *Black on Black Violence:*

> A sense of powerlessness and inter-personal violence are inextricably intertwined. Absolute powerlessness as well as absolute power corrupts. For violence has its breeding ground in impotence and apathy. True, aggression has been so often and so regularly escalated into violence that anyone's discouragement and fear of it can be understood. What is not seen is that the state of powerlessness which leads to apathy which can be produced by the above plans or the uprooting of aggression, is the source of violence. As we make people powerless, we promote their violence rather than its control. Deeds of violence in our society are performed largely by those trying to establish their self-esteem, to defend their self-image and to demonstrate that they too are significant. Regardless of how derailed or wrongly used these motivations may be or how destructive they express it, they are still the manifestation of positive inter-personal needs. We cannot ignore the fact that no matter how difficult their redirection might be, these needs, themselves, are potentially constructive. Violence arises not out of superfluity of power, but out of powerlessness. Violence is the expression of impotence. Having accepted the notion promulgated by his white oppressors - that he will never measure up to their "projected as universal" standards, never be "as good" as they - he vindictively asserts that they will never be as "bad" as he. Thus, he finds near-erotic delight in demonstrating himself as being the "baddest" whoever. In this game he has a better then sporting chance to win; in this game he makes the rules. The essence of the black on black criminal is self-hatred or self-alienation. These can only be learned. Self-hatred can only occur as a result of the self having been made to appear to be hateful, ugly, degrading, rejected, associated with pain, non-existent or devoid of meaning, and adherently inferior. Such appearances and associations are the fruits of American narcissistic racist projection against the African American community.[3]

Why do Black men kill Black men? Because their anger and frustration is displaced. Again Wilson provides the clue:

> Frustration can and does produce a number of consequences of which hostile aggression is only one. Generally, the hostile aggressive reactions to frustrations may be of two types - direct and displaced. Direct hostile aggression refers to the situation where in reactionary aggression is focused directly against the perceived cause and source of frustration. Should the cause or source remain hidden, ambiguous, intangible, or more commonly, so powerful that a hostile, aggressive attack against it would expose the attacker to severely painful retaliatory injuries, deprivation, injurious loss of the various types and possible annihilation, that attack may be redirected towards some object, person, or group other then the original cause or source of frustration. This type of redirected hostile aggression is referred to as displaced hostile aggression. In this instance, the aggressive individual or party, pressed by anger and a compelling need to express that anger yet constrained from expressing it directly finds partial release by attacking a less dangerous target.[4]

Why do Black men kill Black men? Because they are afraid and are not allowed to kill White people. Why do Black men kill Black men? Because that's what they are allowed to do. That's what they are taught to do, and there are few consequences. They are encouraged by being given more guns and lighter sentences.

Sanyika Shakur said that had he lived in a different time, a different place, he could easily have become a Panther, a Nazi, or a member of the JDL. He was a chameleon who could have become whatever the community wanted him to become. I remember when Martin Luther King, Jr. marched on Washington in 1963; there was a reduction of crime that day. Huey Newton and the Black Panther Party presence in Oakland, reduced the levels of crime in those neighborhoods where the Panthers were strongest. When Nelson Mandela first visited New York, there was also a reduction of crime in Brooklyn and Harlem.

There is hope for saving our youth. Our youth are chameleons and they will become whatever we want them to become. Cody Scott, who was once known as "Monster," has now become Sanyika Shakur, and the only variable that changed was culture. Rather then being a Crypt with displaced aggression, he is now a member of the Republic of New Africa who now understands the enemy. The White establishment is cognizant of his consciousness and they have placed him in solitary confinement. As long as he was "Monster," there was complete access to all inmates, so that he could teach them new killing techniques.

In my book, *Hip-Hop versus Maat*, I mention the killing exercise where we asked boys in South Central Los Angeles why they would kill someone. Insane people have many reasons why they would kill someone. Those young people gave us thirty-seven reasons why they would kill someone: he looked at me, he stepped on my shoe, ate one of my french fries, said hello to my lady, I just didn't like him - and they went on and on. Then we asked them, "Of the reasons you would kill for, which ones would you die for?" At that point, they wanted to take back the reasons, but we said, "No. What you would kill for is what you would die for." Sane people usually only have one reason and that is self-defense.

In the last chapter we said that African American men kill themselves with their futures ahead of them while White men kill themselves with their futures behind them. The police often assume that any group of brothers must be a gang, any act of violence has to be gang violence, any crime has to be drug related, and any death has to be homicide. For many African American males, you can't tell the difference between homicide and suicide. Amos Wilson provides the analysis:

> Through committing homicide, the black on black criminal steeped in his existential, internalized white supremacist instigated guilt, often seeks his own death; he desperately searches for his execution. He provokes others

to do desperately searches for his execution. He provokes others to do what he, himself, dares not do - to kill him as a way to kill himself as a way of committing suicide. He is determined that his subliminal guilt must not go unpunished. So he places himself in harm's way. He compels himself to live dangerously. He falls for the ultimate sting. Carrying another man's guilt, he pretends to live without it. He thinks of himself as a black pantherized predator, when in reality he has been chumped into playing the part of a sacrificial lamb.[5]

When African American males drive away from the police in a hundred mile per hour chase and end up driving into a pole, was that an automobile accident or was that suicide? When you have three or four macho brothers who think that they are going to be able to defeat forty gang members in shoot-out, should the police record that as a homicide or a suicide? When an opposing gang member walks in rival gang turf, knowing that there is a war going on, should that be recorded as a homicide or a suicide? When African American males are racing each other down congested expressways at one hundred miles per hour and there is a car crash, should that be recorded as an accident or a suicide? How about the African American males who O.D. on heroin and cocaine? Should those deaths be registered as drug-related or suicide?

A challenging question I get asked a lot is, How do you convince a young person to value long-term gratification when he believes in short-term gratification because he doesn't believe he'll live beyond nineteen years of age? One of the reasons why many middle-class adults have failed in counseling our youth is that they are using the value of long-term gratification when many youth know that their life expectancy is only nineteen years. If you're not confident of living past retirement, you may not want to stay in school learning about Columbus, Lincoln, and Washington. If your life expectancy is only nineteen years, you may not want to work at McDonald's for $4.35 per hour until you die. If your life expectancy is nineteen years, you may not want to save your money and buy a Toyota, Chevrolet, Ford, or Honda when you can steal a Lexus and drive it this weekend.

What do you say to a Monster who is already eighteen and has one more year to live? What do you say to someone who has already tested positively for HIV? I know of a class that was tested for HIV and nearly one-third tested positive. People who hate themselves don't have much compassion for people with whom they are sexually involved with. I have heard White male homosexuals who were angry because they were going to die that they wanted to take as many people as possible to hell with them.

In the final chapter we will look at strategies to reduce the number of "Monsters" from developing; and how we can convert those who do into people like Sanyika.

$\mathcal{C}$HAPTER $\mathcal{F}$IVE

Conclusion

How can we develop an environment where Cody can remain Cody or become Sanyika? How can we reconcile Marlon's Monday morning reality? How can we increase the probability beyond five percent that Jerome graduates from college and either becomes an entrepreneur or is gainfully employed in the area in which he studied? How can we assist mothers raising sons alone?

Over the past two decades, the problems of African American males have escalated, and people often ask me, Do you believe you're making a difference? Do you believe it is possible to save the African American male? My favorite answer always denotes optimism. I still believe that we have more on our side than they have on theirs, that all things are possible for those who love the Lord and are working to achieve His purpose. Presently, we are experiencing a grave Friday night, but there will be a Sunday morning rising. If we give up, we automatically lose. Only if we dare to struggle do we dare to win. The quantitative answer is listed below. Over the past two decades the African American community have developed:

* Over 200 rites of passage programs nationwide
* 1,000 mentoring and role model programs
* Over 100 Black male classrooms
* Three schools with a 90 percent or better African American male population that address their learning styles
* Over 100 conferences about African American men
* Hundreds of workshops to analyze the issues

* Over 30 books written on the subject
* Over 20 colleges that offer scholarships for African American males who want to major in education
* Five states with commissions to address the problems of the African American male
* Project Alpha and The Urban League providing lessons on teenage sexuality and responsibility.

We have done well in our resistance against the destruction of African American males, but the oppressor continues to perservere. The noted educator Barbara Sizemore provides an excellent theoretical paradigm: Problem, Cause, Solution, Implementation.

After reading many books and attending hundreds of workshops and conferences, we know the problems, what caused them, and the solutions. The major question is, What prevents us from moving from theory to practice? Why have we not implemented our solutions? I've listed some of the reasons below: lack of information, time, work, money, Bootstrap Theory, ego, fear, personal problems, lack of consequences, lack of faith, lack of trust, and resistance to change.

Lack of Information

There remains a wide disparity between what the conscious members know and what the masses know. If the masses don't read and will not pay $10-$100 for workshops and conferences and are completely dependent on the mass media for information, how will they be informed?

Time

Many people work eight hours a day, and their commuting time averages two hours. The three meals they eat and the eight hours they sleep leave three hours left in a day. If they choose to spend that time watching television, talking on the telephone, listening to music, playing golf, bowling, working out in the health club, or participating in other recreational and entertainment activities, there may not be time to stop the conspiracy. I suggest everyone chart their twenty-four hours and strive toward giving more hours back to the community.

Work

When we started Community of Men, during our first two months of planning, we had a building full of talkers. In my pastor's manhood class, where all they had to do was sit and listen, the numbers were staggering. But when it was time to *work* in Rites of Passage, Role Model, Mentoring, crime watch groups, junior business leagues, etc., the numbers plummeted. Talk is cheap and work is divine. When people want to talk with me now, I tell them to put it in writing. I tell them to meet me at the Rites of Passage program or at Community of Men. We can talk while we work. I don't mind talking as long as we are combining talk and work.

Money

In order to save our children, we will have to put money on the table. We might have to provide the capital to start the businesses. We may have to buy the T-shirts and provide the money for the bus trips. We may have to finance our youth's business plans. Two of our largest organizations, the NAACP and the Urban League, are both dependent upon outside resources to finance their programs. We can't finance our liberation struggle on grants.

Bootstrap Theory

The Bootstrap Theory, advocated by people like Clarence Thomas, Thomas Sowell, and Shelby Steele, says that you must succeed through your own hard work. All problems can be solved solely with individual effort. Unfortunately, self-help has lately become linked to the Republican party and not African people. The Bootstrap advocates have completely forgotten how their role models and mentors inspired them to be successful. I would like to ask the Bootstrap advocates to imagine themselves as the offspring of a fourteen-year-old mother on crack who never told them she loved them and who made no effort to expose them to successful adults. Would they still be successful?

Ego

The egotistical problems many African American men have working with other men are legendary. Many men are more effective working individually with boys in Little League baseball or Boy Scouts than with groups of men in organizations such as Rites of Passage, Role Model, or crime watch groups.

In our organizations we have a motto: *Leave the ego at the door.* We try to develop all men to be leaders in the organization. One of the ways I evaluate an organization, especially the leader or president, is the level of responsibility he gives to the "lieutenants" and how well the men work together as a team. It defeats the purpose of building manhood when the adults are arguing in front of the boys on who's blacker than who; who speaks more fluent Swahili; who has read the most Black books; who has been to Africa the most; and who's been involved in the liberation struggle the longest.

Fear

The more successful we become at developing Black boys into men the more we become a threat to White male supremacy. In addition to that, many of us are afraid we are going to lose our jobs, contracts, houses, and cars. So we begin to compromise. It has been said that if an African American man gets a good job, you can write him off from the liberation struggle. That the job becomes more important than freedom. My high school history teacher says that our materialism may be incompatible with our quest for freedom.

Personal Problems

Many African Americans are not involved in the liberation struggle because their personal problems have to be resolved. A person cannot be faulted if he is caring for an invalid relative at home, a loved one in the hospital, or a wayward family member who has some deep-seated emotional problems. Can you criticize a brother who can't make the meeting because he has several young children? What if the brother has high blood pressure or prostate cancer?

Lack of Consequences

Teachers are still paid regardless of whether children learn to read. We had 175 men involved in our crime watch group and now we have 21. There were no consequences for the men choosing to do something else or doing nothing. The African American community can strongly suspect that a brother has impregnated a sister but will not hold him accountable for his behavior. Without consequences, the liberation struggle is reduced to people's whims.

Lack of Faith

Deep down in our gut, do we believe? Do we have the faith? Do we have the willpower to believe that we can develop Black boys into men? Have our spirits been so broken that we believe the only boys that we can save are between the ages of five and nine? Do we have enough faith to believe that we can save boys aged nine to thirteen or thirteen to eighteen? The problem with faith is that you can't buy it or discover it intellectually. You either have it or you don't; you either believe or you don't. Scripture teaches, "Faith is the substance of things hoped for, the evidence of things unseen." You don't believe with your ears; you don't smell with your eyes; you don't see with your heart. The only way to believe is to believe with your heart. We have to believe that we can win.

Lack of Trust

If all of us gave one dollar and there are 40 million of us, we would have $40 million. If our 150 largest organizations chose not to meet in White hotels for one year, we would save $16 billion. The problem is, Who would we trust to hold that kind of money?

Resistance to Change

Many Black churches, colleges, and civil rights organizations' favorite slogan is, " This is the way we've always done it." It should be obvious that way is not working. We must identify new ways to save our boys. Why are our boys more committed to the gangs and frats than the Lord and the liberation struggle? What can we learn from gangs to reclaim our boys?

~

Reclaiming our boys will require marathon runners. The race against White supremacy can't be done with sprinters. I am often asked, How long will it take? Slavery in America lasted 246 years, or 12 generations. We have been physically free for 130 years, or six to seven generations. Some people feel it will take another six generations before African people return to the zenith we created in Kemet. I can't speculate on six generations, but on the day of my judgment, I want God to say, "Well done, thou good and faithful servant . . . ."

REFERENCES

Chapter Two

1) *Black Issues in Higher Education*, July 5, 1990, p. 8.
2) Amos Wilson, *Black on Black Violence* (New York: African World Info Systems, 1990), pp. 168-169.

Chapter Three

1) *Black Issues in Higher Education*, July 14, 1994, p. 62.
2) *Black Issues in Higher Education*, May 19, 1994, p. 54.
3) Jacqueline Fleming, *Blacks in College* (San Francisco: Jossey-Bass, 1984), pp.141-145.

Chapter Four

1) Leon Bing, *Do or Die* (New York: Harper Collins, 1991), p. 237.
2) Cody Scott, Monster: *The Autobiography of an L.A. Gang Member*, p. 278.
3) Wilson, op. cit, pp. X, 83.
4) Ibid, p. 129.
5) Ibid, p. 123.